James Augustus Hessey

Church and State Questions in 1876

A Charge Delivered to the Clergy and Churchwardens of the Archdeaconry

of Middlesex

James Augustus Hessey

Church and State Questions in 1876
A Charge Delivered to the Clergy and Churchwardens of the Archdeaconry of Middlesex

ISBN/EAN: 9783337088323

Printed in Europe, USA, Canada, Australia, Japan

Cover: Foto ©Lupo / pixelio.de

More available books at **www.hansebooks.com**

CHURCH AND STATE QUESTIONS IN 1876.

A CHARGE

DELIVERED TO THE

CLERGY AND CHURCHWARDENS

OF THE

ARCHDEACONRY OF MIDDLESEX,

At his Primary Visitation,

HELD AT

St. Paul's, Covent Garden, May 16th, 1876.

BY

JAMES AUGUSTUS HESSEY, D.C.L.,

ARCHDEACON OF MIDDLESEX,

And Preacher to the Hon. Society of Gray's Inn.

LONDON:

JOHN MURRAY, ALBEMARLE STREET.

1876.

My Reverend Brethren, and my Brethren the
Churchwardens of the Archdeaconry of
Middlesex.

It is impossible for any one who has been called to an
office of almost unknown antiquity in the Church Universal,
to enter upon that office without solemn prayer on his own
part, or without entreating the prayers of his fellow-labourers,
both of Clergy and of Laity, that, so far as he is concerned,
" *Ne quid detrimenti capiat Ecclesia.*" Therefore, before I say
one word more, let me assure you that as my own approaches
to the throne of Divine Grace have not been wanting, so I
ask, very earnestly, that I may have the great and inestimable
advantage of your prayers for me being blended with mine.

Your kind reception of me as your Archdeacon has
already given me much encouragement, and, imperfectly as
I know my duties at present, I trust that as years pass on I
may, by God's assistance, be of some little use in my portion
of this vast and overwhelming Diocese. The Archdeaconry
of Middlesex, alone, contains nineteen Rural Deaneries, at
least three hundred and twenty-three Benefices, something
like six hundred Clergy, and a population of certainly a
million and a half.* Under any circumstances, then, I should
need the forbearance and consideration of my brethren in the

---

* The exact amount at the last Census was 1,455,784, and it has
increased since that was taken very considerably.

4

performance of what I have to do with so large a field before
me. But the reputation of many of my predecessors, the
conviction that I cannot equal them even in their individual
excellences, and much less in their united accomplishments,
and the thought that more is expected of those in office now
than was expected heretofore, indefinitely increase that need.
I do not speak of Pre-Reformation worthies, though of them
there were many. But he who occupies the chair of Alexander
Nowell,* the author of the celebrated Catechism, one of the
first-fruits of the Reformation; or of Daniel Waterland,†
whose *Review of the Doctrine of the Eucharist* were of itself
sufficient to brighten the dark days of the eighteenth century;
may be permitted to express some misgiving as to his own
powers. Much more, if he finds that his three immediate
predecessors were a canonist such as William Hale Hale,‡
or a scholar and educationist such as John Lonsdale,§ or,
last but not least in honour, John Sinclair.‖

Yes! John Sinclair! Who, that had the advantage of
personally knowing that venerable man, can forget his kindly
presence, his courteousness, his chastened hilarity, his knowledge of men and of books—always ready to be communicated
to all, but never unduly forced upon any? "*Erat in illo
viro*," says Cicero,¶ speaking of the capturer of Tarentum,
"*comitate condita gravitas;*" and this is my recollection of
our friend's demeanour, whether in private life, or in the
public Societies over which he had to preside, and the internal
storms of which his geniality of temper not unfrequently

* In 1559. Afterwards Dean of St. Paul's and Prolocutor of the Lower
House of Convocation.

† In 1730. He was offered, but declined, the Prolocutorship of the
Lower House of Convocation, and the Bishopric of Llandaff.

‡ In 1840. Afterwards Archdeacon of London.

§ In 1843. Afterwards Bishop of Lichfield.

‖ In 1843. He held the Archdeaconry more than thirty-two years.

¶ *Cic.: de Senectute.*—s. 4.

allayed. To his unflagging energy in the parish committed
to his care, our Bishop has given this striking testimony:—
" During his incumbency he succeeded in adding to it twenty
new churches, with five mission or temporary chapels, besides
rebuilding his own." This last work, be it remembered, was
achieved in his extreme old age, when most men would have
considered that they had well earned some repose. Of his
learned research, of his severely logical reasoning powers—not
unbreathed in the trying schools, first of Edinburgh, and then
of Oxford—and of his judicious application of both to the
requirements of the day and of the Church, his Charges will
be a lasting record. Many of us still remember them as
though they were delivered yesterday. I rejoice to learn that
they are to be republished in a collected form. *The Rights of
Bishops, Presbyters, and the Laity* may still receive illustration
from the Charge of 1864, in these days, when three great
currents of feeling are moving in the heart of the Church,
and somewhat interfering each with the other. These are, as
you know, a desire for an increase of the Episcopate—a
jealousy of too arbitrary interference on the part of Bishops
with the reasonable liberty of Presbyters—an anxiety on the
part of the Laity to be employed in the work of evangelizing,
and to have a voice in the Church's councils, partly welcomed,
partly distrusted by the Presbytery. And the Charge of 1865,
on "Free-thought," contains a *reductio ad absurdum* unequalled,
except by Archbishop Whately's *Historic Doubts relative
to Napoleon Buonaparte*, which is well worthy of re-perusal.
In it his object is to show, that a clergyman who had written
Hume's *Treatise of Human Nature*, or his *Essay on Miracles*,
or his *Posthumous Dialogues on Human Nature*, would be
entitled to acquittal on the very identical grounds on which
Mr. Wilson and Dr. Williams were acquitted. Whether one
agrees with his conclusion or not, it is impossible to withhold
admiration of the ingenuity and delicate irony by which it is
compassed.

You will, I am sure, pardon this passing tribute to Archdeacon Sinclair's memory, and my direction of your attention to the legacy which he has, in his writings, bequeathed to the Church.

I come now to myself, or rather, to my duties in reference to you.

It would be unprofitable, and, indeed, impossible, to enter at length upon the origin or primitive functions of the Archidiaconate, or the particulars of what a London Archdeacon has to do, as compared with what has to be done by his brethren of similar office elsewhere. I will simply say here that, as a Presbyter, delegated by the Bishop, who cantons his diocese into Archdeaconries for its more convenient administration, I accept the old titles of my office, *Episcopi Oculus*, *Episcopi Cor*. By the former I understand, that I am to bring to the Bishop's notice not merely such matters as deserve amendment; but, so far as I may be able, deeds and men who deserve encouragement. By the latter, that I am to represent personally and through the Rural Deans, and other Clergy, and the Churchwardens, the kind and fatherly feeling with which the Bishop regards both the Clergy and the Laity.

From the best enquiries that I have been able to institute, I find that the duties performed or performable by an Archdeacon in this Diocese are divisible into definite and indefinite. The former are those which are enjoined or restrained or permitted, by prescription or by statute, and capable of being executed partly in person, partly by deputy. The latter, those which are more or less optional, and dependent upon personal exertions.

The definite duties of the Archdeacon appear to be:— Examination of Candidates for Holy Orders and Presentation of them to the Bishop for Ordination. Induction of Presentees to Benefices. Holding General Visitations of the Clergy, and Churchwardens, receiving Presentments from the outgoing Churchwardens, and admitting those for the coming year. Visiting Churches and Churchyards, either specially, in consequence of matters which have transpired in Presentments; or, more or less periodically, so as to inform himself as to their condition, and the general Ecclesiastical condition of the Parish. Visiting any Church, or Churchyard, or Parish, at the special desire of the Bishop, to enquire into the reasonableness of any complaints which have been made to him—or into the desirableness of issuing any Faculty, which the Chancellor of the Diocese has submitted to the Bishop for his approval—or into the way in which the terms of a Faculty have been carried out—or to compose, if possible, any Parochial misunderstandings. Administering Funds of which he is an Official Trustee. Attending Meetings for Diocesan purposes at the summons of the Bishop. Preaching certain Sermons at St. Paul's Cathedral where he holds a Stall. And attending the Sittings of Convocation and of its Committees.

Such are the definite duties of the Archdeacon.* I shall enlarge on them presently, because they have been somewhat misunderstood. The indefinite duties it is rather difficult to enumerate. Suffice it to say, that they appear to include membership, and participation in the business, of every large Church Society, whether general or diocesan; constant calls for sermons, to which he responds most willingly, as far as he can; correspondence with the Clergy—especially the younger Clergy, with whom he is happy to advise; and with Churchwardens and many of the Laity. And to these must be added, the keeping himself abreast of the Ecclesiastical questions of the day, and using what influence he can exert to have them exhibited in a light in which their scope and bearing can be best comprehended.

---

* The Archdeacon does not in this Diocese grant Faculties or Marriage Licenses. These powers are exercised by the Bishop. And no Surrogates are appointed by, or in behalf of, the Archdeacon.

Upon many of these, I have, as you know, already entered, and as I am happily free from the cares of a parochial charge, I hope to continue a diligent performance of them.

I proceed to say a few words upon my definite duties:—

On the first, the Examination and Presentation of Candidates for Holy Orders, in which the Bishop kindly allows me to share, I need not dwell; it is a most deeply interesting function, and one which brings the Examiner into close and brotherly contact with the young, to enquire whether they are " apt and meet for their learning and godly conversation, to exercise their ministry duly, to the honour of God and the edifying of His Church." And it is a matter of serious responsibility, to certify, in the presence of God and of the congregation, that one " believes them so to be." I scarcely know a more anxious season than is the Ember Week to all concerned in it. It is a solemn moment, when the youthful candidate, with whom one has prayed, whom one has endeavoured to advise, and with whose weaknesses, it may be, one has become confidentially acquainted, kneels, by one's encouragement and recommendation, before the Bishop, his whole frame sometimes quivering with emotion, showing that even yet

> " The storm is high within
> 'Twixt love of Christ and fear of sin."

But I pass on to another function—that of Induction to Benefices. This is especially one of the duties of the Archdeacon. The Bishop institutes, and then he issues a mandate to the Archdeacon to induct. I think that this duty should, if possible, be done personally. I found, on coming into my office, that a practice had grown up, long before our time, by which, on the Bishop's mandate arriving at my Registry, the Registrar was accustomed to issue, under my seal, and without necessarily informing me what was going on, an Archdeacon's mandate to any Rector or Vicar to induct. For this, a fee is charged of 10s. to the Archdeacon, and of 14s. to the Registrar. The Archdeacon really doing nothing—the Registrar doing what is superfluous—yet both being remunerated. The Rector or Vicar, who actually inducts, receiving nothing—and the Clergyman to be inducted paying what he need not have paid. One or two instances occurred before I knew of the practice; but directly I was informed, I desired that I might always know who was thus coming into the Archdeaconry, that I might welcome him as a brother, and both save him useless expense, and save the Church and her officers the reproach of laying unnecessary burdens upon the Clergy. And my Registrar kindly complied. I shall always, if due notice is given me by a Presentee, be glad to induct him myself, in any parish over which I have jurisdiction. [There are indeed some six or seven ancient Parishes, which, with their modern statutory subordinate Parishes, though locally in the Archdeaconry, are for induction of Clergy and admission of Churchwardens, under the Commissary of London. To these, until the anomaly shall be abolished, and I really do not see why it should be retained, my remarks will not apply.]

There are unfortunately no *Offices* generally authorized by the Church either for Institution or for Induction. Possibly Convocation may take up this subject. A Committee of the Lower House of the Southern Province was appointed on July 9th, 1875, " to consider whether a short *Office* might not be prepared for the Institution and Induction of Ministers, similar to that of the American Church." The Report of this Committee was presented in February last, and again in the present month, amended, but it has not been yet considered by the House. I trust that its issue may be the meeting of a want which is now pressingly felt on occasions so deeply interesting both to Incumbent and to Parishioners. As the Bishops frequently institute publicly, both in this and in other Dioceses, and, as I have said, the Archdeacon is willing to act himself at Inductions, there is no resource at present but to have no Service at all, or to employ a few *Collects* more or less applicable, or to have a form for each Diocese, of imperfect Ecclesiastical obligation, as in the case of consecration of Churches and Churchyards.

I come next to the subject of a gathering like the present. It has, as has been well remarked, a two-fold character.* It is, first, a Court of the Clergy and Churchwardens and Sidesmen or Synodsmen, the business of which is the personal appearance of the Clergy, the exhibition of Articles and Presentments by the Churchwardens as to the state of their Parishes, as to the due performance of Divine Service, and as to the condition of the Churches and Churchyards. And it is, secondly, a Chapter of the Clergy, making with the Laity assembled, a sort of Synod, at which the Archdeacon addresses them upon subjects especially in his province—I mean the moral and material and ritual condition of the Church as distinct from its doctrinal and spiritual matters. These latter are specially retained by the Bishop, who possesses inherently all the visitorial and other official powers of the Archdeacon; and, indeed, reserves them, by an inhibition, for a certain period, in the year in which he holds a personal Visitation. It used to be customary, if occasion required, for counsel to be taken together after the Address. In later times, especially in this Diocese—where the institution of Ruridecanal Chapters prevails, and where the Bishop annually summons the Archdeacons and Rural Deans to a Conference— this custom has been intermitted. The Archdeacon confines himself to suggestions and remarks, which the Clergy consider, at their discretion, in the Ruri-decanal Chapters, or discuss with the Laity in their Parochial Councils. I may state, by the way, that, in modern days, the subjects appropriate to the Archdeacon's Address have become so blended

---

* *See* a Charge, May, 1871, by Archdeacon Harrison, and references there—pp. 6—9, on *Visitation Courts and Synods.*

with others more peculiarly belonging to the Bishop, that the distinction between the characters of their respective Charges cannot always be strictly and sharply observed. It is my desire, however, in anything that I may say, to observe it as much as possible. *Nothing that I shall utter will compromise you.*

Of course, from the very constitution of an Archdeacon's Visitation, the Clergy are expected to be present at it. But, as I know their many engagements, I have most willingly followed the example of the Bishop, and have foregone the custom of calling over their names. But I am always glad to see them, or advise with them, both on such occasions, and elsewhere. Bye and bye, if I am spared to do so, I hope to be more or less acquainted with all. And I may remark that one of my earliest steps was to convene the Rural Deans, as their natural representatives, to a friendly meeting at my house.

The Churchwardens, both the outgoing and the incoming, necessarily appear at my Visitation; the former to make their Presentments, and introduce their successors; the latter to be admitted to office, and to make the requisite declarations. As to both, I may remark that their duties are, I hope, clearly set forth in the paper of *Instructions to Churchwardens,* issued by my predecessor. I have had it very carefully revised by an eminent legal friend; and should any difficulties suggest themselves, I shall be glad to be referred to. Both my Official Principal and my Registrar are ready to give me assistance; though, if a Bill now before Parliament becomes law, I scarcely know how long I shall have them at my side. Their advice I may mention by the way, is, in this Archdeaconry, covered by the legal Visitation Fee of eighteen shillings arranged by the two Archbishops and the Lord Chancellor, and sanctioned by Order in Council. No part of this belongs to the Archdeacon. Two shillings belong to the Official Principal; twelve and sixpence to the Registrar; and three and sixpence to the

Apparitor.* This sum is legally demanded from the Churchwardens. They recoup themselves from the Church Rates,
if there are any: if not, there is seldom any difficulty in its
being defrayed by the Parish. I hope, in spite of the proposal
made in the Bill, that it should be supplanted by a five-
shilling stamp, to be procured and paid for before the Churchwardens are admitted, that things will be allowed to remain in
this respect as they are. For observe: 1st.—The admission of
incoming Churchwardens does not depend upon the payment
of this Fee, and thus no discouragement is offered to their
acceptance of office: 2nd.—The Archdeacon is by means of the
existing charge provided with officers who will give him the
best legal advice, and thus second the moral influence which
he is able to exercise in settling parochial differences, and
questions which, if allowed to proceed further, might involve
considerable expense. It is in consequence of his being thus
fore-armed with the necessary knowledge, that, of late years
at least, scarcely any necessity has arisen for the exercise of
contentious jurisdiction on the part of the Archdeacon. A
vast number of small disputes about seats, and paths in
Churchyards, obstruction of lights, and infringement of
boundaries, and eligibility to serve office, are settled by
reference to him personally. It is only in case of matters
involving serious principles that recourse is had to a higher
court. Civil legislation, indeed, especially the Act for
Abolition of Compulsory Church Rates, has also limited his
contentious jurisdiction : though he still holds a Court to
inquire into any alleged misconduct on the part of a Parish
Clerk, with power of suspension or dismissal.

[And here I would say a word about certain payments
made at Visitations, called " Procurations" and " Synodals."

---

* It is the Apparitor's duty to issue the summonses to the Archdeacon's
Visitation. Somehow or other a great deal of the trouble of doing this had
devolved upon the Rural Deans; of this I have now relieved them, on their
representation, and remitted the task to the proper officer.

It is proposed, by the Bill to which I have alluded, that these should be done away with, compensation being made for them to the present holders of Archdeaconries, though I do not see that the interests of future holders are provided for. They are very ancient payments, and in fact constituted in former days the sole remuneration of some Archdeacons, especially of the Archdeacon of Middlesex.* I care not how soon they are commuted or abolished; and I will tell you why :—

In the First place: Though generally advanced by the Churchwardens at Visitations, they are burdens not upon the Parish, but on the Incumbent or Impropriator, who is liable to reimburse the Churchwardens for them.

Secondly: Though very ancient, and historically connected with the expense supposed to be incurred by the Archdeacon at Visitations, they are, in this Archdeaconry at least, a practical fiction. The Visitation is held at one centre, which is found to be a most convenient method, and involves him in little or no expense.

Thirdly: Besides being a practical fiction, they are a most unfair fiction. Their incidence is very unequal. I will show you how. There are now about 323 Parishes in the Archdeaconry. But of these, after we have deducted what I have described above as Commissary Parishes, and their subdivisions, and subdivisions of the ancient Parishes liable to the payments, there remain only about 43 subject to this impost. The Clergy of all the rest, though in several cases better able to bear the burden, are exempt.

Fourthly: Besides being a burden upon the Clergy, their existence is not quite fair to the Archdeacon, and they are no adequate source of income to him. If every one of them were exacted they would only amount to £24 16s. 6d. per annum. They really average about £18 per annum. And yet his first fruits from them are calculated at £60, as if he

---

* *Archidiaconatus Middlesexiæ cujus victus in Procurationibus consistit.*

still retained under his jurisdiction the Deaneries of Heding-ham, Harlow, and Dunmow, in Essex, and the Branghing Deanery, about one-third of the County of Herts, which were taken away by Order of Council, in 1845, and attached to the Archdeaconries of Colchester, Essex, or St. Albans. The addition of a portion of Kent, and of some peculiars of the Archbishop of Canterbury, and of some Parishes in Surrey, which was made to the Middlesex Archdeaconry, at the same time, in lieu of what was taken away, has caused scarcely an appreciable difference. Some of these Parishes, *i.e.*, all in the Woolwich and Greenwich Deaneries, have, since 1867, been taken away from that of Middlesex and added to that of Rochester. Further changes are yet to be expected when the arrangements for the new See of St. Albans are completed. The main income of the Archdeacon of Middlesex is now provided from other sources, yet he has the annoyance of paying on a partially delusive source of income, and of exacting a payment from his brethren, which is a fiction, and so a grievance—and a grievance unequal in its incidence.

It may be said, that, if abolished, the deficiency in Archdeacons' incomes thus caused, and the first fruits now unfairly paid by them to the Queen Anne's Bounty, would have to be made up from funds now applicable to the aug-mentation of small livings. Commutation may be a fairer method of settling the matter. But, if it is desirable to maintain such payments from the Clergy at all, they should be made more fair in their incidence. And, if they are maintained in their present state, the Ecclesiastical Commis-sioners, or the Commissioners for Queen Anne's Bounty, should be bound to collect them. In the case of Bishops' Procurations, which the Ecclesiastical Commissioners have demanded should be handed over to them, the Bishops and their Registrars have in some Dioceses absolutely declined to collect them, and they have fallen through altogether. In others, the Registrars have collected them, but of course on the receipt of a commission for doing so. We must, however, wait for the further progress of this Bill, though I confess I look upon it with great mistrust. Its avowed object seems strangely different from its main provision. The former is the regulation of Ecclesiastical Offices and Fees, the latter is the supplementing of a Fund to pay an Ecclesiastical Judge, whose decisions seem to have no more finality, and to command no more ready obedience, than those of the Judges into whose room he has succeeded. Expense, indeed, seems to be to a certain extent likely to be limited, in the earlier stages of litigation, and this is something. But if the decisions of the Judge in question are to be made just as liable to appeal as those of his predecessors, or if he considers himself as having no discretion in cases similar to those already ruled by the Privy Council, in some instances without both sides being heard, one scarcely sees that much is gained by the abolition or merging of various offices, some of them of considerable utility, in order to remunerate him.]

I have observed already that the contentious office of the Archdeacon is limited in several respects by civil legislation; so has been the office of Churchwardens. Hence they will remark that in the *Instructions* as to their duties (Sect. 4), and in the *Articles of Enquiry*, no mention is made of their now all but obsolete obligation to present immoral persons, or persons absenting themselves from Church, and the like. And no mention is made of the immense moral good that they may do in the Parishes to which they belong, by high personal character and example, or by seconding the efforts of the Clergyman. The duties which they are specifically still bound to perform are set down in the *Instructions* with sufficient clearness. But I wish to bring to their notice the *dictum* of Lord Stowell (mentioned in Sect. 6), that their office is " an office of observation and complaint, but not of control, with respect to Divine worship."—It is not theirs, whether by custom or by statute, to remove ornaments, or to prevent ritual, which they may deem objectionable; nor, on the other hand, is it theirs, to demand services in the Church, which they may consider necessary; or to insist upon the services being carried out without mutilation or addition. Of course, if they are supported by a vast majority of the Parish, or, at least, of those who are habitually attendant at, or willing to attend at, the Parish Church, their representation would have great weight with their Clergyman. If it does not, their complaint comes before the Ordinary in their return to the *Articles of Enquiry*, and he acts according to his discretion. There is, indeed, another way, permissible under 37 & 38 of Vict. c. 85,* under which complaints may be taken cognizance of. The Archdeacon, or a Churchwarden of a Parish, or any three Parishioners of a Parish, may, under certain limitations of time, as to the things, or acts, or omissions alleged, if they think fit, send in a representation to the Bishop. The Bishop may decide that no proceedings shall be taken. If he does not so decide, he may, by the agreement of the party accused and the party or parties accusing to abide by his decision, determine the matter. If they do not so agree, the question goes to the Court of Arches, now represented by the new Ecclesiastical Judge, from whence an appeal lies to Her Majesty in Council.

Such are the provisions of this new Act, which was expected to do great things, but which, I believe, will effect very little. It will effect very little, because a decision by the Bishop, with the consent of the parties, will be simply *in personam*, not *in rem*. It will not prevent exactly the same question from being raised in other places.

And if a decision is given by the Court of Arches, it is liable to be reversed by the Superior Court, and at present, on a number of points raised, or liable to be raised, the Court

---

* Commonly called the *Public Worship Regulation Act*.

of Arches feels itself bound by the existing decisions of the Superior Court.

For these reasons, I should, as Archdeacon, consider very maturely, before I endeavoured to put the provisions of the Act in motion. And I should not merely advise a Church-warden and any three Parishioners, but earnestly exhort them, to pause, before they adopted a course which, after all, is not compulsory upon them, but purely optional. And yet more, supposing that some association external to a Parish had, with whatever pretext, and with what theological bias soever, induced some three Parishioners to send up a repre-sentation to the Bishop, complaining of matters with which the Parish and Congregation generally are satisfied, I should recommend the Churchwardens, and those who are so satisfied, to take means to let the real state of the case be known to their chief Pastor. And, having made it known, to add a petition that he will pause also. It may be said, perhaps, pause till when? I reply, in some cases, until by movement from some other place, where persons are not so judicious, not so large-hearted as themselves, the points in debate have been reconsidered, and after mature argument on both sides, decided one way or the other. In most cases pause altogether. And let no one be startled at this recommendation. (We are speaking, as does the Act, of external matters, not of doctrines.) It is not worldly, but Scriptural. It is not latitudinarian, but catholic. It is not founded on political considerations, but deep in human nature. Above all, it is essentially practical and charitable. And let me tell you why I say this: If there ever was an unworldly man, both in his personal conduct, and in his advice to others, it was St. Paul. His proceedings with regard to the circumcision of Timothy, and his advice of forbearance to the Corinthians in reference to eating meat offered to idols, and to the observance of holy days may be studied by us with advantage. We are fond of looking back to the days of early Christianity. Well, we find

B

great diversities in worship and shades even of doctrine endured then without serious interruption of harmony. It is as impossible to make all persons think alike on the accompaniments of Divine Service, as it is to induce all men to admire the same landscape, or to pursue the same method of arranging their domestic affairs. God has bestowed upon us many great and excellent gifts; let, then, all be employed to His honour. He has given us a variety of tastes, and a variety of objects to call them forth. Colour, and harmony, and voice, and proportion, and form, are all of them His. We possess or appreciate them respectively in different degrees, and should not be offended if some of us bring one or other of them more prominently forward than we ourselves do. I may illustrate what I mean by a consideration which I have employed elsewhere. I had an opportunity, some time ago, of visiting a room in a School of Art, where a number of students were occupied in drawing. They were all copying the same object, a model of a cathedral. All of them were advanced draughtsmen, and little fault, I was assured by the teacher, could be found with the perspective of their performances. And yet no two of their drawings were alike. In one the choir or chancel was most prominent; in another, the spire; in another, the nave concealed the chancel altogether; in another, the whole building appeared, though, even here, projections threw parts of it into deep shadow. Of course the reason of this was that no two of them could, from their allotted places, nearer or further off, in the front or at either side, on the floor, or in a gallery against the walls of the apartment, obtain exactly the same view. Each took the cathedral from his own position, and accordingly transferred a modified idea of it to his cartoon. And yet there was similarity enough, even in the most different representations, to convince me that the object copied must have been one and the same.

It struck me at the time that this might serve as a sort of

parable of the compatibility of a general grasp of truth, with considerable variety of opinion, in members of the same Church. One man, it seemed to me, might be awed and impressed with the greatness of the grace conferred in Baptism, another with the fear of indolently reposing on that grace. One with the importance of laying hold on Christ by faith, another with the necessity of evidencing his Christianity in his life. One with the importance of Holy Orders as a Divine Commission, another with the obligation to improve the grace of God thus conferred. One with the great blessedness of frequent Communion in the Holy Eucharist, another with the great blessedness of Prayer, or the read or preached Word, and the like. Each person might seize upon any one of these as his dominant idea, without being supposed to neglect the others." *

This illustration may, I think, be extended, and applied to our present purpose. So long as the body of worship remains the same, and so long as symbolism, or " teaching by the eye," as it is sometimes called, or the attitudes and accompaniments, employed, *are fairly within the Church's rubrical allowance, and do not necessarily and of their very nature inculcate something contrary to her teaching*, we should charitably bear and forbear. *Unless they come under this canon I have not a word to say for them.* But there is a greater approximation to each other in the various schools of which the Church consists than we believe, so long as we shut ourselves up in our own limits, or trust to reports in vehement periodicals.

Let me further explain what I mean, premising that I use the designations which I employ simply for the sake of clearness, not to convey any reproach. Perhaps the Broadest Church in London has a musical service as attractive as that which is furnished by the very Highest. Perhaps the " Seven Words"

---

* See *Boyle Lectures*, Second Series, pp. 172, 173.

which several of the latter class supply, may find their parallel in others to which no obloquy attaches. Perhaps—nay, certainly—the prominence given to our Blessed Lord's Atonement, was, during the days of our Home Revival Missions, equal in some of the most Ritualistic Churches to that which is given to it in the most Evangelical. And some words which I have just read in a letter by one of the ablest of the Evangelical School are very remarkable. He had been explaining his reasons for restoring his Parish Church, and distinguishing carefully between excess and defect in matters of ritual and ornament, and a due and legitimate employment of them. Then he proceeds. "There is, I believe, no surer way of promoting such abuses than denying or ignoring the truths and excellence that underlie them. Error, it must be remembered, is almost always the exaggeration of some truth. Superstition itself, even in its grossest forms, is the excess of fear or zeal in matters of religion. The fault is not attention to religion, but attention to it in a wrong way. And the person who is most likely to arrive at a just conclusion is the one who has a mind large enough to discover where the germ of truth lies, and in what consists the error, which has grown as an incrustation around it.

"It is the opposite course which has frequently been productive of much harm. Men are easily driven from one extreme to another. There is a notable instance of this, in the fact that many of those who have of late adopted the practices of Rome were originally brought up in a totally different school of thought. They have been urged in this direction by many culpable neglects which they have observed; such as irreverence in worship, depreciation of the Sacraments, and the undervaluing of due order and discipline.

"On their account we should be anxious to supply all that their minds may legitimately require; we should remove any occasion for well-grounded complaint, and never give the least pretext for their excesses by reason of our defects.

"And on our own account we should be on our guard, lest we let slip that which might be very conducive to our spiritual health, and the want of which is fraught with a danger of its own.

"I do not deny that there may be a love of ornamented service where there is no true love of Christ, and that outward ceremonies may be the mere mocking substitutes for spiritual realities; yet, on the other hand, a very plain service may be an equally dead thing, and the man who plumes himself upon being 'no Ritualist,' may, nevertheless, be 'no worshipper.'"

For these reasons, again, I recommend you to pause before putting the Act into operation. A little more forbearance and a little more discretion on all hands would bring us more closely together, and render it almost unnecessary. If those of each school would but compare their own works with those done by others they would discover even a greater approximation than I have already alluded to.* Though under different names, they would find every spiritual age, and every spiritual want, and every need of the poor, and every circumstance in his career, provided for—every class exhorted and encouraged to do its duty to other classes— every yearning of our nature, in its best moments, to spend and be spent for Christ's sake, developed by opportunities for action. What matters it, though different names are used, if, by any means, Christ is preached and the body of Christ is edified? It would be premature to anticipate the proceedings of Convocation in the matter of revising the Rubrics, under Her Majesty's Commission; but I may at least say that everything which has been agreed to hitherto, is directed towards comprehension, and the avoidance of favour to any particular school.

---

* I have been led to this conclusion by a careful examination and comparison of Pastoral Letters, and annual statements of work, social, moral and spiritual, issued by Clergy, of very different shades of opinion, to their Parishioners.

As to visiting Churches and Churchyards more or less periodically. This is generally performed through the Rural Deans, according to the Bishop's Commission. It was to be done yearly, but the Bishop has now, at the request of the Rural Deans of Middlesex, revised the Commission, and once at least in four years has been substituted for yearly. I hope frequently to accompany them, as my brother Archdeacon has done in London.

At their request also, I have drawn up a printed form of Report, which will make their inspection more systematic, and save a great deal of that trouble in writing, which is evident in one laborious Report which I have received. All their Reports will be transmitted by me to the Bishop. Various parishes I have visited already informally, either on my own motion, or at the invitation of the Clergyman or Churchwardens, or at the desire of the Bishop. And I need hardly say that anything that has transpired at this General Visitation, or that appears in the Reports of the Rural Deans, will receive anxious attention. With regard to Churchyards, I shall have something more to say before I conclude. As to those which are disused, perhaps the recent Faculty issued by the Chancellor of the Diocese with regard to a certain Churchyard in the East of London, may suggest a method of making them both ornamental and available for quiet recreation. Of course it will be understood that, in such cases, the question in Sect. 16, of the *Articles of Enquiry*, is answerable in the affirmative: "Is fit attention paid to the decent preservation of Monuments and Graves?" As to those which are still in use, the tenour of the Resolutions which have been recently rejected by both Houses of Parliament, but which are sure to be represented by a Bill, either this year or next year, demands our candid consideration. By *candid*, I mean deliberate weighing our inclination to admit them—not merely our inclination to reject them. We may err in the former as well as in the latter way. Perhaps, from the local circumstances of many of the Parishes in this Archdeaconry, we are more likely to err in the former way.

[There are two Funds for the benefit of the Clergy, of which the Archdeacon of Middlesex is an Official Trustee. As their exact character is not generally known, I mention them here. The first is a Fund established by Bishop Porteus, in 1808, for Clergy officiating in the *then* Diocese of London, and which is therefore available still for Clergy of London, Middlesex, Essex, and the old Archdeaconry of St. Albans, who may be, from lack of means, in distress. It is in amount £219 per annum, and is distributed, in the month of February in each year, in grants, generally of not more than £10 each, two only of £20 being lawful in the same year. The other, called " the Rev. Dr. George Richards' Charity for the Relief of Infirm Clergymen," established in 1850, is of a larger amount—about £600 per annum. This is distributed twice a year, in the months of February and July, in grants of not less than £50 or more than £100 each, to Clergymen throughout England and Wales. The recipients are those who, though of fair means, may need some temporary aid, in circumstances of sickness or overwork, and by it be enabled to get medical relief, or change of climate, or relaxation, so as to be recruited for their labours. I am sorry to say that there are many applicants for both. Whatever information is required with respect to the latter, with the necessary form for application, will be readily supplied by Mr. George H. Brooks, of 7, Godliman Street, Doctors' Commons. With respect to the former, by the Archdeacon within whose limits the Clergyman applying is permanently officiating. Mere residence within an Archdeaconry, I may mention, to prevent misunderstanding, is not a sufficient qualification.

The Trustees of the Bishop Porteus' Fund, are the Archdeacons of London, Middlesex, Essex, Colchester, and Rochester and St. Albans.

The Trustees of Dr. Richards' Charity are the above five Archdeacons, the Vicar of St. Martin's in the Fields, and the Preacher of the Charterhouse.]

I need not dwell on the rest of my definite duties—already mentioned—or indeed, upon the majority of my indefinite duties; I will only say that I perform, and will perform them, by God's help, to the best of my power. And I again thank both the Clergy and the Laity for having accepted so kindly what I have endeavoured to do thus far.

It remains that I make some remarks upon three questions of the day which are of very pressing importance.

The first of them arises out of the 44th Section of the *Articles of Enquiry*:—"Is a printed copy of the Table of the Degrees prohibited in Marriage publicly set up in the Church?" (Canon 99).

The second, from the 11th and 12th Sections:—" Is the Churchyard properly fenced and kept in good order?" " To whom by custom, or by law, are these matters chargeable?" " Is it kept free from all improper uses?"

The third is a matter of general policy which it is impossible to ignore. What should the Clergy do in the circumstances of discouragement which attach in this Archdeaconry, especially in that part of it which falls within the Metropolitan area, to the maintenance of Church Education for the poor?

I feel bound to offer to you some observations on each of these points. I will condense them as much as I can.

An attempt is being made this Session to induce the Legislature, by an indirect process, to render valid a connection*—I cannot call it a marriage—of a man with his wife's sister. If this is brought about, I need scarcely point out to you that the Table of Forbidden Marriages, which is

---

* By enabling children of such unions contracted in the Colonies to succeed to property in the Mother Country.

authorised by the Church, will be infringed upon in one point.
But it is more important to observe that, by such infringement,
its authority upon all points will be impaired. It will be impossible to maintain the Table as founded on Scripture, which
indeed it is throughout, either in the letter or by inference and
implication, unless it is accepted in its entirety. And to this
must be added the consideration that embarrassment will be
caused to the Clergy, who will naturally hesitate to admit to
the Holy Communion, those who are not, according to the
view of the Church, united in lawful marriage. You know
how the miserable question arose. That connection, and,
indeed, all those which are mentioned in the Table, were
originally voidable by the Ecclesiastical Law, if action was
taken during the lifetime of both the parties. If proceedings
were not taken during that period they could not be taken
afterwards, and thus the issue was by mere lapse of time
rendered legitimate for civil purposes. The Church's discipline
slept, and it was seldom worth anybody's while to interfere,
unless some worldly interest was at stake. At length exactly
such a case appeared. A connection of this particular descrip-
tion occurred in a certain noble family. Serious complications
involving title and property might have ensued. On this, an
Act was passed, which, while it seemed to be called forth by the
scandals produced by such connections and the injury accruing
to the offspring, had really a very different object, the relief of
the special offenders. They were supposed to have acted in
ignorance of the law, or through mistake as to the meaning
of voidability, and were, therefore, forsooth, to have their connection legalised. This, however, was studiously veiled by
legalising, not merely *their* connection, and the issue from it,
but every such connection which had taken place, or should
take place, up to a certain date. After that date, in order
that there might henceforth be no mistake, no plea of ignorance whatever, such unions were to be absolutely void and
null from the beginning. It was thus presumed that people

would for the future take warning. But mark the mischief of what may, without irreverence, be called "respect of persons." Almost immediately after that Act had been passed, and a principle had been broken in upon for the sake of relieving certain great people, other people began, frequently in defiance of the entreaties of friends, to break the law. Their contention was that it could not be a Divine law, or it would never have been allowed by the human legislature to be contravened. Accordingly they set on foot an unceasing agitation, without regard to difficulty or expense, to get it repealed. For years they have carried this agitation on. In vain has it been shown to them, over and over again, that the Table which the Statute sanctions is part of the Moral Law. In vain, that it was understood so to be by the Church Universal, until, towards the end of the fifteenth century, Alexander VI. (Roderic Borgia) gave a dispensation for the union of Emmanuel, King of Portugal, with his sister-in-law, following it up afterwards with a dispensation to Ferdinand, King of Sicily, for a union with his own aunt. In vain are they reminded that, though from the sixth to the fifteenth century, the Tables of Forbidden Degrees were much extended, and though such additional prohibitions were frequently dispensed with, and the Church of Rome has chosen in her infallibility to confound all prohibitions together, and so at length to claim power to dispense with all; the latter are purely Ecclesiastical, those in the Table are Moral. At first she only dispensed with the additional Ecclesiastical prohibitions, and did so on the ground that they were not Moral but Ecclesiastical. In vain have their professions that this is *the one* case of hardship been exposed, by their being reminded that it was originally proposed to sanction a union between a man and his niece, but that this was abandoned as being too shocking to the moral sense to be endured.

In vain has the plea that the law must be bad because it

has been often violated, been refuted—1st, By documentary evidence that even worse transgression against the Tables has been committed; and, 2nd, By showing the absurdity of the admission of a principle which would render it necessary to repeal any law against which there are frequent offences.

In vain has it been proved to demonstration that this question is not a poor man's question. Their assertion that it is so has been disposed of by statistics which show that the majority of such unions have taken place among the lower portion of the middle class, with a few among the upper.

In vain has their assertion that it—the union—is not forbidden in Scripture in so many words, and that nothing not so forbidden is unallowable, been disposed of by the following argument, which shows that implication and fair inference must be admissible :—

Firstly.—It is not *said* that a father may not marry his daughter. We *infer* that to be unlawful thus : it is said that a son may not marry his mother ; conversely, we *infer* that a mother may not marry her son ; and then, by analogy, we *infer* that a father may not marry his daughter. But this is a prohibition by inference; it is not found in so many words.

Secondly.—It is not *said* that an uncle may not marry his niece. We *infer* that to be unlawful thus: it is said that a nephew may not marry his aunt ; conversely, we *infer* that an aunt may not marry her nephew ; and then, by analogy, we *infer* that an uncle may not marry his niece.

Thirdly.—In the same way, *it is inferred* that the marriage of a man with his wife's sister is unlawful. It is *said* that a woman may not marry her husband's brother ; and this case is *exactly analogous* to the prohibition of a man's marriage to his wife's sister.

Those, therefore, who will admit nothing but what is set down in so many words to be Scripture, are brought to this : they must either allow all these inferences, or none of them ;

i.e., if they allow a man to marry his wife's sister, they must allow an uncle to marry his niece, and even a father to marry his daughter.*

In vain has it been shown that Lev. xviii. 18, which, at first sight, appears to sanction it, has, when rightly interpreted, (as it is in the margin of the Bibles†), nothing to do with the matter, but is, probably, a precept against polygamy.

In vain has the futility of the plea that the gentleness of an aunt will modify the proverbial harshness of a step-mother been exposed; and it has been shown that, even supposing this would be so in a few cases, it would be a very small compensation for impairing the now unsuspected and affectionate relations existing between every man and his wife's family.

In vain has it been shown that—granting that Protestant bodies on the Continent, and the Church of Rome allow such unions—it has not been proved that family relationships are thereby rendered more happy, or marriages more sacred.

In vain have legal decisions, one after another, disallowed such unions, quashed the plea of ignorance of the law which is still urged, and overruled the alleged hardship to children, by the obvious reply that it is unfair that those who have voluntarily created the hardship should look to the State for redress, and wound the conscience of the Church by the redress being granted.

And, in vain, year after year, has Parliament declined to change the law.

The agitation still goes on; and it has now assumed the following form:—Acts have been passed in the Parliament of

---

* See *Argument against permitting Marriage with a Deceased Wife's Sister*, being a pamphlet by the Author, called a *Clergyman's Letter to a Friend*. Rivingtons.

† The marginal reading is, *one wife to another*.

Australia, where Church feeling is, of course, not so strong, legalising, so far as they could go, such unions. The Home Government, after considerable hesitation, has allowed these Acts to become law, on the ground that they were portions of Colonial domestic policy. The result is, that the children of such unions, being rendered legitimate there, desire to be considered legitimate in the Mother Country as well; and this demand is eagerly supported by the favourers of such unions here. I commend to your careful consideration, the statesmanlike reply of Lord Carnarvon:—"He did not consider the deputation were justified, in consequence of certain Colonial Statutes having been passed, in asking Parliament to rescind its expressed opinion and to go back from its policy. If their request were granted the result would be that the Colonial Parliament had nothing to do but to pass Acts within a certain province of legislation, and the Mother Country, in order to avoid a discrepancy on the subject, would have to change its legislation so as to conform with that of the Colonies." And I entreat you to continue your resistance to every effort, whether direct or indirect, to do away with a restriction founded deeply in our moral nature, exhibited in Scripture as part of the Moral Law, recognised as such by the whole Church for 1,500 years—happily still so recognised by our own Church, when we separated from Rome, and of inestimable importance towards the maintenance of purity and affection in our social relations. Is such a point to be surrendered at the bidding of a Society, which has never shown itself to the light, except by the name of a Secretary and by a firm of Solicitors, and which is really a disguise assumed by a few rich men, who have wilfully broken the Statute with which they desire to do away?

I now come to the question—a very serious one—How far are we justified in conceding a demand which is now being made that services other than those of the Church of England should be permitted in our Churchyards?

Let us, first, unequivocally understand what is the exact issue before us.

It is not whether we will allow Nonconformists, who are Parishioners, to be buried in our Churchyards. This claim we are not inclined to disallow, impaired though it is as a claim of strict justice by their freedom from liability to maintain the Churchyards.

It is not whether the Clergy of the Church of England will use the Church Service at the burial of Nonconformists. This they already do, if the person whose body is brought to be buried was baptized with water in the Name of the Trinity.

It is not whether we will carry animosities with Nonconformists beyond the grave, and symbolize an opinion uncharitably imputed to us, that they cannot be united to us in the resurrection of the body, by refusing to be united to them in the corruption of the body. We neither assert, nor desire to symbolize, any opinion of that kind.

Our view is simply this, and it is well that it should be laid down with all the distinctness possible :

We hold that the State has, as a matter of fact, recognised the Church of England as the depositary of Christ's teaching in this country, and that the Ecclesiastical edifices of the Church of England, and the Churchyards locally or otherwise connected with them, are in her keeping, and are to be used for and with her Services exclusively.

We hold, in accordance with these positions, that all who claim the benefit of such Ecclesiastical edifices and Churchyards, should be content with her Services, which are not legitimate unless celebrated by her own Ministers.

We hold, (for we admit the validity of Baptisms in certain cases, though they may not have been performed by a Minister of the Church of England), that any one, Nonconformist though he be, who has been baptized with water in the Name of the Trinity, has a claim to be buried with such

Services, and by her Ministers, unless he have forfeited it by having died formally excommunicate, or by having been pronounced a deliberate suicide.

We hold that, in strictest justice, those who possess this claim to be buried in our Churchyards should be bound to abandon it, if they assert and enjoy an immunity from the expense of maintaining them. We do not, indeed, press such abandonment. But we hold that, if they do urge their claim to be buried there, and, if we concede their manifestly impaired claim, they should either accept our Services and Ministrations, or not injure our discipline and wound our consciences by intruding others which we consider unauthorized, and which, we fear, may lead to irreverence.

We hold, further, that no real grievance is endured by Nonconformists. In fact, we more than suspect the specious cry for "religious equality in the grave" to be rather a political watchword, proclaimed by a few, with an ulterior and aggressive aim, than an expression of anything like a conscientious yearning to be freed from a hardship.

All these positions the Nonconformists, or rather, those who profess to represent them, dispute.

We, of the Church of England, though persuaded that equity, and even the strictest justice are on our side, are naturally anxious to promote peace and quietness. Accordingly, various methods of arrangement have been attempted by us. I do not mean, of course, that they have been publicly offered, but that they have been offered with sufficient distinctness to exhibit our willingness to meet any reasonable allegation of inconvenience or unfairness.

But we have not received the slightest encouragement. On the contrary, it has been epigrammatically said of our overtures, that Churchmen will offer nothing that Nonconformists will condescend to accept.

A clever saying, however, is hardly conclusive of a matter. Very often it is capable of being met by a rejoinder. And this is the case here. It may be said quite as pointedly, and with much more justice: Nonconformists will accept nothing which Churchmen can concede, having due regard to their existing position, or to the fiscal burdens binding upon them, or to common prudence in the presence of their adversaries' avowed aims, or to their feelings of reverence, or to their conscience. The only compromise which the Nonconformists will enter upon is one which involves an unreserved surrender of Churchmen's rights. There is, forsooth, to be no reciprocity whatever. The others have nothing to do but to demand; Churchmen have nothing to do but to yield. They are to be content with the issue of the contest, though it be like that described by the Roman satirist—

"Ubi tu pulsas, ego vapulo tantum."

The following may serve as specimens of compromises, proposed, on our part, with more or less authority, which have been promptly, not to say scornfully, rejected. One of them, perhaps, goes beyond what the majority of Churchmen would be willing to concede, but its even partial entertainment shows that a conciliatory spirit exists strongly and un-mistakably amongst us.

Would you be satisfied with a silent interment—our Ministers doing nothing but simply registering the fact of the burial in the Parish books?

The answer has been, No.

Would you be satisfied if our Ministers used a Service over the body, consisting merely of passages of Scripture, so as not to offend the scruples of the religious Society to which the deceased belonged?

The answer has been, No.

Would you be satisfied, if we allowed recognised Non-conformist Ministers to officiate, with a prescribed form, consisting of Holy Scriptures, Prayers, and Hymns, our object in laying down these restrictions being to prevent irreligious or infidel demonstrations?

The answer has been, *No.*

Would you be satisfied, as you claim to be buried in Churchyards, to submit to a re-imposition of compulsory payment of Church Rates, and thus to let things be as they were?

The answer has been, *No.*

Would you be satisfied, if, though we tax ourselves already for the maintenance of Churchyards, an impost from which you are now freed, we were to tax ourselves additionally, by a general rate, in order to purchase and keep up Cemeteries.

The answer has been, *No.*

Thus all these overtures have met with a rebuff; and a recent Resolution on the subject, in the House of Commons, which we may presume expresses the determination of those who profess to represent the demands of the Nonconformists, is this:—

" That the Parish Churchyards of England and Wales, having been by the common law of England appropriated to the use of the entire body of the Parishioners, it is just and right, while making proper provision for the maintenance of order and decency, to permit interments in such Churchyards either without any burial services or with burial services other than those of the Church of England, and performed by persons other than the Ministers of that Church."

For the present this Resolution has been defeated in the House of Commons, as has been a similar one in the House of Lords. But they, or some Bill involving them, are sure to be brought forward again.

What is to be done?

I am afraid that it is all but useless to lay before the self-constituted asserters of what they call the rights of the Nonconformists, the arguments by which the unreasonableness of their demands may be shown.

But we may remind ourselves of them, and lay them in a clear form before those who are amenable to reason.

Such are the following :—

1. A common law right to be buried, if it exists, is surely to be accompanied by a common law obligation to maintain the Burial Ground. Those who have been freed from the latter have little reason to complain if they forfeit the former.

2. The Nonconformists were freed from the burden of Church Rates, because it was against their consciences to contribute to the maintenance of Churches and Churchyards. Desecration, which Churchmen declare would take place, if services other than those of the Church are permitted, is certainly against the Churchman's conscience. Nonconformists have declined to accept a proposal that recognised Ministers of their respective bodies, and decent forms only should be admitted. And various recorded funerals of Infidels and Socialists show what *may* take place. Should not then the consciences of Churchmen be respected, on the ground that they may feel desecration at least as much as the others feel a pecuniary burden? And especially as they sustain themselves the pecuniary burden of maintaining the places which they are requested to submit to the chance of desecration?

3. If the Nonconformists have any real grievance at being obliged to accept the performance of the Church's service by a Minister of the Church of England as a condition of being buried in the Churchyard,—

How is it,

That this was not brought forward when the compulsory payment was put an end to?

How is it,

That, where Churchyards and Burial Grounds belonging to Nonconformists exist in the same Parish, the friends of deceased Nonconformists so frequently prefer the former to the latter?

How is it,

That the cry of grievance has usually arisen, not in the

country, where the resource of Cemeteries does not exist, but in towns where that resource does exist?

How is it,

That the fact is utterly ignored—that the grievance, if there is one, is being reduced year by year, as Church-yards are closed for sanitary reasons, and will shortly be minimised?

How is it,

That Nonconformists, including the two extremes of Romanists and Quakers, who happen to have Burial Grounds of their own, decline to admit any services but those belonging to their sect, or not opposed to it?

Besides, if Churchmen were to claim to be buried there, would they not be told that they did not contribute to their maintenance? Why, then, is a similar reply not permissible in reference to Churchyards?

How is it forgotten,

That, if the consciences of any men require relief in the matter, they are the consciences of the Clergy, who are com-pelled, because a person has been baptized with water and in the Name of the Trinity, to bury him with the rites of the Church? He may have been vehement throughout his life against her doctrines and ordinances, or he may, as indeed many professing Church people may, have lived anything but a godly life; but his relatives think a Church funeral respectable; though he has practically put himself out of the Church's pale, he is presumed to have been reconciled, *in articulo mortis*, and so has a right to her ministrations.

How can it escape observation,

That, if we concede the claim to unconditional use of the Churchyard, now that Church Rates are not compulsorily payable to support it, it is difficult to see how we can resist a demand for unconditional use of the Church. It is absurd to meet this by saying, "A man need not go to Church, but he must be buried." The cases are not similar. For, as I have stated already above, the grievance is practically *nil*—it was never alleged till recently—it is in process of being remedied by the creation of Cemeteries. Moreover, it is scarcely to be doubted that the Church would, for peace and quietness' sake, allow silent burials, so far as the Churchyard is concerned, the relatives celebrating, or causing to be celebrated, a service accordant with their own views, elsewhere.

While those who profess to represent the Nonconformists ignore all these considerations, it must, I fear, be impossible to meet them on equal grounds.

We are told that we are judging uncharitably of the state of the dead. Why, we are doing nothing of the sort. We are willing to celebrate a Service in all charity, but we decline to allow the terms of our Communion to be violated.

We are told that we shall strengthen the Church by concession. Surely this is a strange plea when urged by those who, almost in the same breath, express their intention of disestablishing the Church. Those who are defending a castle, must be pardoned if they do not see the wisdom of surrendering the outworks, and if they decline to accept the assurance of the besiegers that they will be contented to proceed no further.

But the question recurs,—

What is to be done?

Let us frankly state,

That we cannot allow our own conscientious scruples to be over-ridden in order to satisfy the consciences of other people.

That we cannot shut our eyes to the designs of those who take their consciences—or rather, the alleged consciences of other persons—as a vantage-ground for an attack upon the Church.

That, as all conditions have been rejected, we must resist the unconditional admission of Nonconformist Ministers, and Nonconformist Services, into our Churchyards.

But, at the same time,

That we do not wish to spare our purses by alleging our consciences. And, accordingly, that we are ready, wherever such a resource does not already exist, to promote the acquirement of Cemeteries, and to perform our part in bearing the burden of their acquirement and maintenance.

That we are ready to do this, everywhere, in order to remove any possible future ground of complaint. That we are ready to do it, even where there is a sufficiency of room in the Churchyard, and where the relatives of Nonconformists have hitherto made no objection to their friends being buried with the Church's rites, and by the Church's Ministers.

That we are willing to have a measure to the above effect passed at once.

That meanwhile, and indeed for the future, we should not object to either of the following sorts of burials taking place in our Churchyards.

A burial, of the body of a person baptized with water in the name of the Trinity, at which the Church's Minister shall officiate, without taking the body into the Church, and the *Office* for which shall consist solely of passages from Scripture. Whether such a burial can be extended to children of baptized persons, dying unbaptized without their own fault, (on the principle supposed to be sanctioned by 1 Cor., vii. 14,) who are already granted, though by no direct order, a silent interment, is a matter open to consideration. I very much think it might; a plain reason for this extension being found in our wish to refrain from pronouncing upon the state of the dead, and to comfort their surviving friends in their sorrow. Or, if it should be undesirable to have such an *Office* at the grave, it might still be possible, *after* the burial, for the Church's Minister to hold, in the Church, under *the Act of Uniformity Amendment Act*, a Service with the mourners.

A burial, with regard to which, so far as rites in the

Church and the Churchyard are concerned, no Service is employed. It cannot be said that this is a proposal on the *Church's* part to give a man the burial of an animal. Those who use a Service of their own elsewhere than at the grave, as Presbyterians and Roman Catholics, prevent its being so. Those who use no Service at all, can accuse no one but themselves, if they make it so. And it cannot be said that such a burial is necessarily contumelious because wilful suicides are entitled to it. For, first, such burial of such persons was enforced by the State, to prevent the indecency of the former method of burying them in the public road, at a time when no other decent burial-place existed than the Churchyard. And, secondly, the burial of which I speak here, would be one conceded, in her charity, by the Church, to the demands, reasonable or unreasonable, of those who desire it. And, if the proposal of a general rate for Cemeteries is adopted, it will be of very rare occurrence indeed.

I could not satisfy myself without making these remarks. Some of us—*amongst these I include myself*—were inclined, until it was discovered that all attempts at conciliation were fruitless, to go further than I have now ventured to advise. And, perhaps, where, as in the thickly inhabited parts of this Archdeaconry, for which, from sanitary considerations, Cemeteries are provided, we live exempt from the annoyance of having our Churchyards intruded upon, and our Orders set at naught, and our Services disallowed, it was not unnatural that we should incline to concede even unreasonable demands. Perhaps, too, a pardonable excess of candour may have induced us to listen too trustingly to a plea advanced by English Nonconformists, when incontrovertible statistics had shown that they at least had no real grievance. This plea is that their non-conforming brethren in Wales are subject to a sort of hardship; that in Wales Nonconformity prevails to a great extent, and that the general feeling is against the Church, and her Services, and Ministers.* And hence that they cannot, on principle and in honour, avoid taking up their brethren's cry for relief. We may reply, Well, granting this to be so, why not limit your demand for relief to the case of Wales? Why not join in a petition, not for participation in Churchyards there, but for the remedy which we are willing to assent to—a general burial rate, accompanied, if need be, with powers to compel sale of land for Cemeteries? But what if, after all, the grievance alleged is infinitesimal, and Nonconformist Burial Grounds exist in Wales, to an amount which fully meets their need, if they choose to use them? This is said to be the case. Besides, if you, on principle, contend for the cause of others, may not we, on principle also, contend for our own cause? And if the topic of honour is to come in, I do not see why those Churchmen who, from being provided with Cemeteries would not feel any inconvenience from the intrusion of Nonconformist Ministers and Services into their Churchyards, should not sympathise with those of their brethren who would feel that inconvenience very much. On the whole, I cannot help thinking that the plea thus urged is a resource adopted as a last ground of attack, when others have proved to be untenable. Of this I am sure, the eyes of many have been opened by the failure of all efforts at negociation. An excellent friend of mine—now, alas! a late friend, for he has been called to his rest and his reward—told me that he attended a meeting of Clergy and Nonconformists in order to try whether any fair basis of agreement could be adopted. He went to it with the utmost wish to concede. He was not what is called a High Churchman, in fact, quite the reverse. But he assured me that he was obliged to abandon the attempt in despair. All or nothing was the *ultimatum*.

---

* A friend of mine, very well acquainted with Wales, informs me that whatever may be the feeling of the Welsh against the Church, they do, in many places, make a great point of obtaining her Services for Marriages and Funerals.

I have scarcely left myself time to treat of the one remaining subject which I proposed to bring before you—the difficulties experienced by the Clergy in maintaining Church Schools. These have always been considerable, but they are greatly increased since the passing of the Education Act.* I do not speak, however, of the chronic indisposition of people to give at all, but of difficulties of recent creation to which that Act has mainly given birth. Putting them generally, they may be classed under the following heads:—

Where there is a Board School actually in a Parish.

Where there is a Board School, not actually in a Parish, but very close upon it—*viz.*, in some contiguous Parish.

Where there is a Board School threatened in a Parish, which already possesses a Church School of some capacity, indeed, but not of sufficient capacity, or not with buildings that will satisfy Government requirements, or where the Parishioners are unable or unwilling to enlarge and improve it.

Where a sufficient Church School, with buildings, &c., exists, but the Parish refusing or being unable to contribute to its maintenance, it is found impossible to keep it up with efficiency.

These difficulties, again, will be varied in their character and magnitude according as the Parish is within or without the Metropolitan area. In the one case the Parishioners are now burdened with a Rate which they cannot escape, and are, therefore, unless very good reasons are shown to them, unwilling to submit any longer to a voluntary impost. In the other, there is generally found a considerable proportion of persons hostile or indifferent to religion altogether, who are glad to avail themselves of the opportunity of escaping any burden—or, of persons, who are opposed to Church teaching, and disposed to accept any teaching but that of the Church.

I am not inclined to assert, for a moment, that an

* Of 1870, amended in 1873.

Education Act of some kind or other was unnecessary. It was, I think, very necessary that something should be done to meet the following facts, with which we were confronted at every turn:—The fact that vast numbers of children, in various parts of the country, and especially in large cities and towns, were not reached by the existing machinery of education, on the part either of the Church or of Nonconformist bodies. The fact that vast numbers of people, well able to bear such a burden, denied or escaped the duty of assisting in the education of the poor. Hence the necessity of an Act. And hence came—though I do not consider it to be the best and fairest* that could have been passed—this Act. I accept it; and, though I would fain amend it in some of its details, I am not disposed to recommend any movement on the part of Churchmen for its abolition. Such a movement would be wrongly interpreted. It would be stigmatized as a deliberate approbation of what was formerly merely acquiesced in *per incuriam*—*viz.*, of leaving many absolutely uneducated, and of freeing many from the responsibility to educate. And, besides this, it would be to attempt an impossibility. The Act has been for nearly six years in operation, and it has, by the bodies which it has called into existence, by the buildings which it has erected, and by reason of the public mind having become accustomed to it, forced its way into the constitution of the country. In regard to it, the nation is much in the condition of the steed mentioned by Horace, who, you will recollect—

" Non equitem dorso, non frenum depulit ore,"

and it cannot get rid of it. I must add—it would not, I fear, if it could.

---

* The Act was not fair to the Church, whose endeavours to overtake by education the increase of population had been much greater than those of all the Nonconformists taken together. It was therefore only due to her that she should have received distinct and marked encouragement, instead of being classed with those who were satisfied with an imperfect religious training, or were willing to dispense with religion altogether.

It is, however, quite another thing to consider what should be done by the Church in the presence of this Act— that is, how to make the best of what we do not altogether approve. For instance, to consider whether, where School Boards exist, what is injurious in their action cannot be, to a certain extent, neutralized? Whether, (and there is some encouragement to hope for this in the recent refusal of the House of Commons to make the establishment of School Boards universal,) they cannot be, in many more cases than we at present suppose, averted. Whether within the School Boards themselves much may not be done to prevent education from being altogether secular, by insisting upon some religious, though not distinctively Church, teaching. And, lastly, whether both with consistency and with justice, the provisions of the Act may not be modified. By the phrase *with consistency*, I mean that I would press for no modification which is not in accordance with its main principles, that every one who is able to bear such a burden, should be rated for the support of education, and that every one should be educated. By *with justice*, I mean that the burden should be so regulated, that its incidence should not operate unfairly upon either the consciences or the pecuniary resources of any of the community. At present, in reference to this latter point, it obviously contravenes the professed intention of its authors and promoters, and of many who acquiesced in its enactment. It supplants, instead of merely supplementing, the educational efforts not only of the Church, but of various non-conforming bodies. These, wherever its provisions are in operation, unless they will endure an education either absolutely and purely secular, or, at best, free from denominational bias, are obliged to submit to an impost twice over. Such an obligation they consider to be very hard, and more than hard, to be inequitable.

I will first suppose, for the moment, that things are to remain just as they are, or, in other words, that the Act is to be left, even in its minutest details, unmodified, and that no steps are to be taken to modify it. And I will approach the cases above mentioned in order.

1. What is a Clergyman to do, if a Board School already exists in his Parish? Such a Board School either ignores religious teaching altogether, or professes what is called undenominational religious teaching. Whichever line is taken by it, his duty surely is to induce his Parishioners to help him in his endeavours to impart some Church education, that is, to provide some place in which it may be imparted. Two methods, by which this may be provided, suggest themselves. A Mission House may be built and supported, or for Sunday School teaching the premises belonging to the Board School may be rented. Of course this will cost money, but encouragement in effecting either object is given, in necessitous cases, by the Bishop of London's Fund, in this Diocese, and by the Christian Knowledge Society, and the National Society, and the Church Sunday School Institute, both in this Diocese, and throughout the country. The Clergyman is thus able to represent to his Parishioners that, though they are burdened with a Board School rate, the voluntary burden will not be so very overwhelming; that surely they will endure it rather than allow the children of the poor to grow up without knowledge of God and hereafter, which would be the result of mere secular teaching; and that, if the Church's teaching is of any value to themselves—that is, if they know why they are Churchmen—they will see the importance of proceeding further than to undenominational religion. And his exhortations will receive additional weight from his being able to show that those who are without are impressed with a sense of the gravity of the effort which he desires them to make, by coming liberally to their aid. I cannot help imagining that there will be instances in which (I am speaking here of Parishes external to the Metropolitan area) the earnestness of the Clergyman will so far infect the

Parishioners, that a vast majority of his people will submit their children to the Church's teaching in the hours proposed. It is possible, too, at least outside the Metropolitan area, that there will be instances in which, in consequence of other Denominationalists doing, in their own way, much the same thing, a vigorous reaction will take place in favour of Denominational Schools; that premises will be acquired for them, the premises of the Board School abandoned, and the precept for establishing a School Board become a dead letter. What I have said here will, of course, not be applicable to Parishes within the Metropolitan area. The extreme pressure of the Act must remain there, unless such modifications of it as I shall suggest bye and bye are brought about.*

2. But what if a Board School exists in a contiguous Parish, drawing off the children of a clergyman's own Parish, or exhibiting, by the efficiency of its teaching, so far as it goes, or by its accommodation and educational appliances, an appearance which places his Church School at a disadvantage. Here, again, the Clergyman will have to urge arguments upon his Parishioners much like those which I supposed just now, only he will have to urge them with *greater* earnestness and pertinacity. This will be necessary— 1st, Because religious evils are less felt in one's neighbour's

---

* I read as follows in a report of the Salisbury Diocesan Synod. "On the education question his Lordship observed that he intended to consider it at length upon the occasion of his approaching Visitation, but could not refrain from mentioning in passing that in several instances in the Diocese School Boards seemed to be in a very inert condition, and in other cases the rates had been so increased that the afflicted Parishes acted as standing advertisements of the evil of School Boards. His Lordship urged the Clergy and School Trustees not to surrender their freehold rights in their National Schools."— *Bishop of Salisbury's Speech*, April, 1876. It is true that at present no provision is found in the Education Act under which a School Board can be dissolved where it is no longer wanted; or where the educational wants of a place can be more efficiently met by other means, and the ratepayers would make the change if they could. But this is an additional reason for making every effort to keep out a School Board in the first instance.

case than in one's own; 2nd, Because they cannot help seeing, if in the Metropolitan area, that they are bearing two burdens, while their neighbours have, or may have, only one; 3rd, Because almost everywhere there are persons, who, though preferring Church teaching, do not distinctly enough know why they prefer it, to endure paying twice over. Such a position is very hard to contend with.* But it may be, in a great measure, met by an exhibition on the part of the Clergyman of zeal and devotion, and personal labour in the work of Church education. This must eventually affect the best of his flock. They will be induced to help him in raising the tone of the secular as well as of the religious instruction in his school, and also in improving its material condition. Here I may mention a point which is worth considering, in reference both to this case and to others. May not the children's fee for schooling in Church Schools be raised? It was placed at its present low rate when wages were much lower than they are now. Parents would be quite able to bear an advance. This would greatly lighten the Clergyman's difficulty.

3. But what if there is a Parish in which there is already a Church School of some capacity, but not of sufficient capacity, or not with buildings which will satisfy Government requirements, or where the Parishioners are unable or unwilling to make it what it should be? A School Board either exists, or is talked of, and threatened. A Board School is looming in the near distance.

This is a difficult case, whether the Parish is within or whether it is without the Metropolitan area. If it is *within*, arguments and exertions, such as have been recommended

---

* "It will become every year more difficult to obtain subscriptions, as the subscriber feels he is being rather hardly dealt with, for by subscribing to the Voluntary School he is doing two things : one thing that he heartily approves of—helping education ; and another, saving the pocket of his more stingy neighbour, which he does not so much approve of or wish to do."— *Speech of Mr. W. E. Forster, M.P.*, Nov., 1875.

already, must be employed. If it is *without*, no pains must be spared to induce the Parishioners to improve their present building, and to bring their educational appliances up to the required standard. They should be shown, by statistics, carefully prepared, but yet sufficiently simple, that not merely will the Parish have to incur a greater expense* in the aggregate than it has now, in erecting and maintaining a Board School, but the very individuals who now contribute voluntarily, and who are vexed at their neighbours declining to contribute, will find their quota of contribution increased. To encourage them, help might, perhaps, be obtained from the sources already mentioned, and from such a Church Association as exists in several of the Rural Deaneries. And they may thus be prevailed upon to avert the impending evil. If all this is found ineffectual, I fear that, under the present provisions of the Act, a School Board must come, and then the circumstances mentioned in Case 1 will have to be met. A noble instance, indeed, has occurred in this Archdeaconry, by which a School Board has been averted. A Parish just outside the Metropolitan area was threatened with one, and must have succumbed;—but a neighbouring Parish, itself in this area, and already pressed with a double burden, stepped in, and not merely helped to build, but promised a yearly subsidy for the maintenance of, a Church School. .

4. What if a Church School, with sufficient buildings, &c., already exists, but by reason of a large proportion of the Parishioners refusing to contribute to its maintenance, it is found impossible to keep it up with efficiency, and if thus the formation of a School Board has been ordered?

Then a resource exists. The Church School buildings may be let to the School Board, under condition of their being available for Church teaching at certain hours; and the

* See a pamphlet by Canon Gregory, entitled, *The Cost of Voluntary Schools and of Board Schools.* Published by the National Society, Sanctuary, Westminster, 1875.

expense will be very greatly lessened to the Church Parishioners. The National Society provides forms under which
this letting may be effected.* It must be remembered, however,
that it is not incumbent on any School Board to make such
an arrangement, and that, even if made, it is only valid until
the next triennial election. Therefore, as great efforts must
have been made by the electors to return members who would
be favourable to it, in the first instance, so, great efforts must
be made at every election, if the arrangements adopted by the
previously existing Board are to be continued. In all cases,
indeed where School Boards exist, constant vigilance is
required on the part of the electors who care for the interest—
I will not say of the Church—but of religion. A majority
of one may convert a Board from the Undenominational
system of religious teaching—which, though unsatisfactory,
is far better than nothing—to mere secular teaching. This
latter brings up children with a view to the present world
only, and produces a hardness of heart with which it is almost
impossible to combat. The former is a postponement, indeed,
of doctrinal teaching—it is as it were, putting off the full
educational training in Christianity, which the Church desires
all her children to go through, to a later period than is
desirable,—but it supplies an acquaintance with the Bible
upon which such training may be engrafted; and though it
does not adequately inform the mind, it is calculated to keep
the heart open for the reception of the more advanced Christian
truths, in their due and just proportions. Only one caution
more is required in this case. It is not incumbent upon any
Parish to surrender either the freehold or the leasehold of its
Church School to a School Board, either originally, or at the

* *Forms of Indenture*, and *Articles of Agreement*, can be had at the
Office of the National Society, Sanctuary, Westminster. But an important
*Circular from the Committee of the National Society to the Managers of
Schools in Union, adopted at a Meeting held on the 2nd of June, 1875, His
Grace the Archbishop of Canterbury in the Chair*, should be carefully
studied.

end of a triennial period. It may be shut up, or used for other purposes. But no process exists by which its surrender to the Board can be enforced.

Thus much for working under the Education Act of 1870, supposing it to remain exactly as it is. But might not its two leading principles—that every child should be brought under education, and that every one capable of contributing to the cost of education should be rated for that purpose—be preserved intact, while at the same time some modifications of its provisions is attempted? This I believe might be done. And the result of doing it would be that much of what renders the Act unpopular would be satisfactorily removed. As to the manner in which it might be done, a suggestion of great value is derivable from the system now pursued in Lower Canada, which may be described in the words of the Bishop of Manchester, then Mr. Fraser. I quote these words from a most able pamphlet on the subject, by Canon Gregory :* "In Lower Canada, whenever in any municipality the regulations and arrangements made by the Commissioners of any school are not agreeable to *any number whatever* of the inhabitants professing a religious faith different from that of the majority of the inhabitants of such municipality, the inhabitants so dissentient may collectively signify, in writing, such dissent to the Chairman of the Commissioners, and give in the names of three trustees chosen by them (for three years, one retiring each year,) which trustees shall have all the powers and be subject to all the duties of School Commissioners, for the purpose of establishing and managing dissentient Schools. They become a corporation, they constitute their own school districts, have the sole right of fixing and collecting the assessments to be levied on the dissentient inhabitants ; are entitled to receive, out of the General School Fund appro-

* *Is the Canadian System of Education Rates possible in England?* By ROBERT GREGORY, M.A., Canon of St. Paul's, &c. Published by the National Society, Sanctuary, Westminster, 1875. Price 6d.

priated to the municipality, a share bearing the same proportion to the whole sum allotted as the number of children attending School at the same time in the municipality, and a similar share of the building fund."

Surely something like this might be adopted among ourselves. Most of our hardships would then disappear. Every one would be rated for education, once and once only. Every one who preferred Undenominational religious teaching could obtain it in the Board Schools. If any one wished for something less than Undenominational religion, *viz.*, Secularism, he might be protected by a conscience clause. There would scarcely be more than four religious bodies who would desire to have separate Schools, *viz.*: the Church of England, the Wesleyan Methodists, the Roman Catholics, and the Jews. All, or nearly all the rest, would fall in with the system of the Board Schools. Indeed they have already generally done so, and have thus avoided the double expense which presses so hardly on their brother Denominationalists. Every parent would be able to get his child educated, but would be freed from the temptation to sacrifice his religious convictions in order to do so.

Of course it would be necessary to frame various precautionary clauses in order to ensure the availableness of such a modification of the provisions of the Education Act, or, in other words, to engraft upon it, to any good purpose, the system of Lower Canada. Every parent should not merely be allowed to choose the School to which he desired to send his child, but should be statutorily compelled to send his child to some School. The expenses of each School would have to be accurately regulated, and the allocation of subsidies out of the general rate to be carefully adjusted. General Education Boards in behalf of each Denomination, as well as a General Board in behalf of Undenominational or Secular Schools, (if Secular Schools continue to exist), all of them subject to the Educational Committee of the Privy Council,

D

would have to be constituted. These, however, are matters of detail, for which I would again refer you to Canon Gregory's pamphlet. It is impossible to do more than allude to them here.

I used the expression just now, "if Secular Schools continue to exist," and I used it most advisedly. It may be doubted whether the country will long endure Schools which are absolutely secular, *i.e.*, the principle of which is godless. At any rate this does not seem to be the wish of Mr. W. E. Forster, M.P., who conducted the "Education Act" through the House of Commons. And it is very noteworthy that his speech, delivered at North Tawton, scarcely a month ago, contains a remarkable admission that it is impossible to educate religiously without a creed, in fact without something like a body of doctrine.* He pauses, indeed, at a point far

---

* After other observations Mr. Forster spoke as follows, and he appears to have carried with him the approbation and even the applause of his audience. "They were also very anxious for this, and they ought to be anxious for it, that no advantage should be taken of their need and desire for education, and, above all, for religious education, to swell the numbers of one denomination and one sect rather than another; and consequently there was a jealousy—a well founded, most reasonable, and just jealousy—against any kind of attempt at Schools, and by reason of Schools, to obtain advantage for one denomination at the expense of another—either of Church over Dissent, or Dissent over Church. Lord Portsmouth, and their Vicar, and he, and no doubt the Dissenting Ministers of the place, had all united together, and what had happened was this—that in their School they insist upon reading the Bible, and not merely upon reading it, but upon teaching it. They insisted upon learning the Belief, the Apostles' Creed, the Commandments, and man's duty to God and his neighbour, the first part of the Church Catechism, to which no one could object. The final result had been that they had no religious difficulty whatever. On the contrary, had they done otherwise, they would have had religious difficulty he ventured to say. He should not have been there that day and Lord Portsmouth's money would have been wasted if they had attempted to establish a Boarding School upon the Secular system, or even a Day School. A Boarding School upon the Secular system was an absurdity, because the master occupied the place of the parent, and how could he hope to obtain moral and religious control over the children to whom he stood as parent without being allowed to give them religious instruction? But as they had worked it they had had no difficulty, and,

short of the Church's full teaching. But it is a something to have gathered from the lips of one who is a keen observer of the religious pulse of the country, and a candid and religious man. Language of a similar character was used by Earl Fortescue, at Barnstaple.*

The utterances of both these eminent persons are satisfactory in their general effect. And it is to be observed that they seem to go further than to prefer Undenominational teaching to Secularism. Mr. Forster speaks in so many words

---

therefore, he went away from this School with an additional confirmation of what he had long held, that the religious difficulty was one made by controversialists outside the real work of education, and disappeared as soon as men set to work to get a School upon principles which actuated parents generally in England, and disappeared because they set to work to give them that kind of religious instruction in which all could unite and which all desired for their children."—*Times*, April 20th, 1876.

* Earl Fortescue said, "He had never varied in the opinion that the Education Act of 1870, although in many respects valuable, was imperfect, and that it was not creditable to England as a Christian nation that instruction in the primary principles of Christianity, upon which all sects were agreed, should be left to the option of the different School Boards, and that all testing of religious knowledge by the Government inspectors, who so severely tested secular knowledge, should be given up. The latter practice had been very satisfactorily carried out for many years, and he believed it worked extremely well. The opinion he originally formed, that the Legislature did abandon one of what he considered to be its positive duties as a Christian Legislature, had since been strengthened. He had no sympathy at all with those who would ignore the rights of conscience, but he thought it a great misfortune that the instruction of children in the general doctrines of Christianity should be abandoned by the State. He said that the more confidently because for something like a quarter of a century the British and Foreign School Society had been proving conclusively that what seemed to Parliament and to municipal bodies to be very difficult was practically not only feasible, but easy, and had been systematically carried out for a long period. He had himself been present at examinations in Scriptural knowledge conducted successfully by dignitaries of the Church of England and eminent Nonconformist ministers at the central establishment of the Society he had named, and he could only say that the amount of knowledge of the Bible, and especially of the Testament, which was shown by the scholars on that occasion was most gratifying and surprising even to those who had entered the room with a high standard of expectation. He had made this statement before, and he did not hesitate to reiterate it, because he could not help trusting that the enormous preponderance of Christianity over all the recog-

of " the Belief, the Apostles' Creed, the Commandments, and man's duty to God and his neighbour, the first part of the Church Catechism," as things "to which no one can object." Earl Fortescue's language tends the same way. This, I say, is more than to prefer Undenominational teaching; it is to advance towards doctrinal teaching, and to leave the Church less to do in the impartation of her own teaching to complete it.* It will not, however, justify our giving up our Church Schools; for it does not even mention Baptism as a Sacra-

---

nized forms of religion in this country afforded grounds for hoping that in some future time the error in judgment, rather than deliberate purpose, of ignoring Christianity might be remedied by the Legislature, and because meanwhile, though in the enormous majority of cases the School Boards of the country had required a more or less Scriptural instruction to be given in Schools; yet in one town at least it had been forbidden, and the efforts of voluntary teachers, zealous as they were, had been found quite unequal to the task of supplying any Scriptural instruction whatever. He was afraid separate instruction by a separate set of teachers—regular teachers being forbidden to impart any Scriptural or religious instruction—could not but be carried on at great disadvantage. The melancholy fact remained, as he had said, that in Birmingham there was at the present moment a very large number of children who were instructed in secular knowledge of various kinds, but who were absolutely left in ignorance, so far as regarded any teaching beyond that given at home of all Scriptural knowledge. For these reasons he was glad to see the success which the public teachers had attained. His Lordship subsequentlydistributed the Prayer-book prizes given out of a fund left by the late Bishop of Exeter."—*Times*, April 21st, 1876.

* Some remarks having been made in the *Guardian* upon Mr. Forster's speech, that gentleman wrote an explanatory letter to the following effect:—

" *To the Editor of the ' Guardian.'*

"Sir,—My attention having been drawn to your notice of what I said at the North Tawton School a few days ago, will you allow me to correct a misapprehension?

" In describing and approving the religious education given at that school (which I may observe is a Voluntary Middle-class School, and chiefly for boarders), my reference to the first part of the Catechism was intended to apply only to what is taught in the school, viz., the Apostles' Creed, and the child's duty to God and his neighbour.

" April 30th, 1876." "W. E. FORSTER.

On this the Editor observes:—

" We quoted from the *Times:* but we understood the passage in the sense in which Mr. Forster now explains it, and which appears to us to entirely

ment;* it says nothing of the Sacrament of the Lord's
Supper, nothing of the Ministry, nothing of Confirmation,
nothing of the Church itself.

I will only observe in conclusion, that, as an alternative
for the engrafting on the Education Act the system of Lower
Canada, a proposal of another modification of it has been
widely, though privately, circulated. It is in the form of a
suggestion of a plan for retaining both education rates and
voluntary subscriptions by an equitable plan of adjustment.†
Its reasonableness is set forth by the same considerations
which justify, or would justify, an adoption of the system of
which I have been speaking: the unfairness that some are
now taxed doubly, while others are taxed once only ; and the
hardship, that while those who do not care especially for any
one form of religion are gently treated, those who do feel an
attachment to their particular belief are not thought of at all.
To this, however, is added another point, which, as it could
not have been entertained at the time of the passing of the
Act of 1870, ought, under the change of circumstances, to
be entertained now. It is this:—The arrears of School
Building are now nearly made up. The Education question
has entered upon a new phase. It is not now one of *building*
but of *maintaining*. Therefore, there should be a double
Education Rate. One to repay the loans for the building of
Board Schools, wherever they exist—from which no one
should be exempt; another, a Rate for maintaining Schools,
which all, indeed, should be subject to, but the amount

cover our argument against the exclusion of the Apostles' Creed from Board
Schools."

I need hardly state that the admission of even as much as the Apostles'
Creed in Board School teaching is, as I have said in the text of the Charge,
an advance in doctrinal teaching from mere Undenominationalism.

* It will be remembered that the word *Sacrament* does not appear in the
first part of the Catechism, which alone is mentioned by Mr. Forster.

† The title of this Paper is *Education Rate and Subscription. Suggestions
for Plan of Adjustment.*

of which falling upon any individual, should admit of a
certain reduction, if he is a subscriber to a Denominational
School. As in the other case, great care and delicacy would
be necessary in order to adapt this proposal to the Act. But
(in the words of the Paper that I have alluded to) "the Act
of 1870 was carried in the name of Justice, amid loud
proclamations of the rights of Conscience. By such a
readjustment of the burden of School Maintenance, for
Town Districts at least, as has been suggested in this proposal,
loyalty would be shown both to Justice and to Conscience,
a real grievance would be entirely removed, and a solid
foundation would be laid for lasting peace and goodwill
between the supporters of Board Schools and Voluntary
Schools." In places where School Boards do not already
exist, all managers of Schools will be put upon their mettle
to keep them out. One Rate, a compulsory one, will, of
course, be levied, but everyone will be able to turn that into
a Denominational subscription. It will be the fault of Churchmen and other Denominationalists, if they cannot so far
compose their differences by conscience clauses as to obviate
the necessity of a second Rate for an Undenominational, i.e., a
Board School. Of course, also, it must be made imperative
upon every parent to submit his children to some education, and imperative on certain authorities to see that he
does so. Which of these two modifications of the Act (if
either) the Government is about to propose, I have no
means of knowing. But I earnestly commend the consideration of the whole subject to you, as Christian Ministers
anxious to promote all practical harmony if not of thought
yet of action, as just citizens desirous to remove all grounds
of discontent and sense of unfairness, as thoughtful politicians,
careful to get imposts paid with cheerfulness; and, as good
economists, concerned that imposts to be paid should be as small,
and that imposts actually paid should be expended as frugally,
as possible. At present there is an expenditure for Board

Schools which we cannot help fearing is sometimes incurred for competition's sake, and to draw attention to the commodity supplied, rather than required by the necessity of the case. There is a taxation which presses very heavily even upon those who approve of Board Schools, and very heavily indeed upon those who earnestly value the tenets of their own Denomination. There is a constraint upon conscience in localities where a Board School is the only means of education. All these are considerable evils. May we have wisdom to remedy them, for the promotion of peace on earth and goodwill towards men, and (through the attainment of these) of glory to God in the highest. AMEN.